The
Mysterious Secrets of
DREAMS

Carl R. Green and William R. Sanford

 Enslow Publishers, Inc.
40 Industrial Road
Box 398
Berkeley Heights, NJ 07922
USA
http://www.enslow.com

Original edition published as *The Mystery of Dreams* in 1993.

Library of Congress Cataloging-in-Publication Data

Green, Carl R.
   The mysterious secrets of dreams / Carl R. Green and William R. Sanford ; illustrated by Gerald Kelley.
      p. cm. — (Investigating the unknown)
   Rev. ed. of: The mystery of dreams.
   Summary: "Explores dreams, including why we dream, what causes dreams, the various meanings and symbols of dreams, and how dreams can relate to our actual lives"—Provided by publisher.
   Includes bibliographical references (p.   ) and index.
   ISBN 978-0-7660-3821-9
   1. Dreams—Juvenile literature. 2. Dream interpretation—Juvenile literature. 3. Fortune-telling by dreams—Juvenile literature. I. Sanford, William R. (William Reynolds), 1927– II. Kelley, Gerald. III. Green, Carl R. Mystery of dreams. IV. Title.
   BF1091.G74 2012
   154.6'3—dc22   2010039687

Paperback ISBN 978-1-59845-306-5

Printed in China
052011 Leo Paper Group, Heshan City, Guangdong, China
10 9 8 7 6 5 4 3 2 1

To Our Readers: We have done our best to make sure all Internet addresses in this book were active and appropriate when we went to press. However, the author and the publisher have no control over and assume no liability for the material available on those Internet sites or on other Web sites they may link to. Any comments or suggestions can be sent by e-mail to comments@enslow.com or to the address on the back cover.

Illustration Credits: Allan Hobson / Photo Researchers, Inc., p. 19; The Granger Collection, New York, p. 13; © ISM / Phototake, p. 22; Jeremy Walker / Photo Researchers, Inc., p. 30; © Jordan Simeonov / istockphoto.com, p. 16; NASA / Ames Research Center, p. 17; © 2010 Photos.com, a division of Getty Images, p. 15; Science Source / Photo Researchers, Inc., p. 20; Shutterstock.com, pp. 1, 4, 6, 23, 32, 33; © Warner Bros. / Everett Collection, p. 9.

Original Illustrations: © 2010 Gerald Kelley, www.geraldkelley.com, pp. 8, 27, 35, 36–37, 40, 42.

Cover Illustration: Shutterstock.com (Woman sleeping with night sky).

Contents

Authors' Note   5

1. This Theater Is Open Every Night   6

2. Dreaming Through History   12

3. Messages From Behind Locked Doors   18

4. Dreams and the Psychic World   25

5. Making Sense of Your Dreams   31

6. A Dreamcatching Expedition   39

Chapter Notes   44

Glossary   46

Further Reading
(Books and Internet Addresses)   47

Index   48

Authors' Note

Thanks to science, many of nature's great mysteries have been solved. Do you want to know more about earthquakes or earthworms? There's probably an expert somewhere who can answer most of your questions. But wouldn't this be a boring world if we knew all there is to know? Perhaps that's why people want to believe that the mind does possess mysterious powers.

In this series, you'll learn about these mysteries of the unknown:

- ✦ *The Mystery of Fortune-Telling*
- ✦ *Astonishing Mind Powers*
- ✦ *The Mysterious Secrets of Dreams*
- ✦ *Amazing Out-of-Body Experiences*
- ✦ *Discovering Past Lives*
- ✦ *Sensing the Unknown*

This book will introduce you to the role dreams can play in your life. Do these nightly mini-dramas have something useful to tell you? Do they foretell the future? Are they a channel for ESP? Once you read about the role dreams play in your life, you can make up your own mind. Perhaps you, too, will decide to become an expert at capturing and analyzing your dreams—a dreamcatcher.

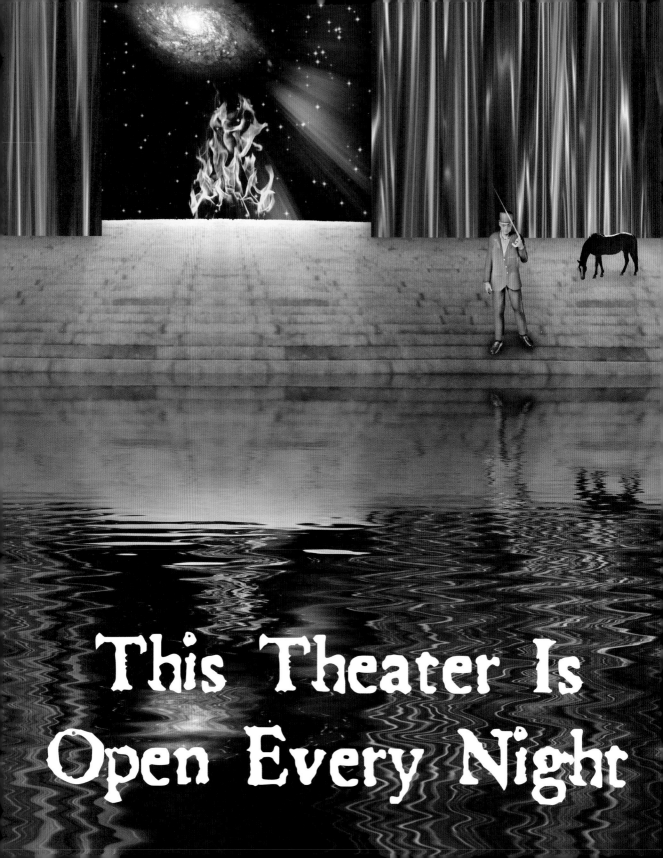

This Theater Is Open Every Night

Do you admire the authors who write great stories? Believe it or not, you are a great writer, too. Night after night, you make up wonderful tales of mystery and adventure. Sometimes those stories are still fresh and alive when you wake up. "Oh," you groan, "It was only a dream!"

Ten-year-old Perry is the "baby" of a large family. Now that he's growing up, he wants to play a bigger role in family affairs. In his dreams, if not in real life, he can have his wish. Here is a dream that lets Perry feel important:

> Last night I dreamed I was at a carnival. They let me shoot cardboard ducks with a gun. I got them all. The man said, "He's the best shot of all. Give him one hundred ice cream cones."[1]

Thanks to his dream, Perry feels like a "big shot." But many dreams are filled with more puzzling clues. Have you dreamed of soaring high in the sky? Flying dreams often leave you feeling "on top of the world." Then comes the night when a sharp-fanged monster pursues you. You wake up with your heart pounding, a scream tearing at your throat. At times like that you might wish you did not dream at all. But research shows that dreams are as much a part of your life as breathing.

Each of us dreams—every night. That is true even though you wake up and say, "I did *not* dream last night." A more truthful statement

Perry is the youngest child in his large family, but he does not want to be treated like a baby. That wish comes true in shooting gallery dreams that make him feel like a "big shot."

would be, "I can't remember my dreams from last night." In eight hours of sleep, you may spend up to two hours dreaming. Most dreams are short, but a few screen as "feature-length" dramas. Dream events take about the same time to "happen" as they would in real life. Do you dream in color? Most people do—but only about one-third of the time.[2]

Dream researchers have collected thousands of dreams. They find that like films, dreams can cut quickly from scene to scene. Many focus

Dream researchers believe that like films, dreams cut quickly from scene to scene. Dreams also make for popular topics in movies. The 2010 movie *Inception*, starring Leonardo DiCaprio (left), is based on a story about technology that lets the user invade another person's dreams.

Useful Definitions

Researchers who study the mind have defined a number of key terms that refer to the role dreams play in our lives.

dream—A series of thoughts, feelings, and images created by the mind during sleep. Many dream scenes are taken from data stored in the unconscious mind.

dream analysis—The process of finding meaning in your dreams. No matter how weird a dream may seem, analysis may help you find its hidden meaning.

dream symbol—A dream image that often hides its true meaning. For example, the black-and-white monster that chases someone in a dream is a symbol. It might stand for the fear that a student musician feels as the yearly piano recital draws near.

latent content—The hidden meaning of a dream. For example, someone may dream that his bike is falling apart—but he does not own a bike! As he studies the dream, he senses that it may relate to a friendship that has been going through some rocky times.

manifest content—Dream messages that can be taken at face value. For example, someone may dream that she turned in a blank test paper to her math teacher. The dream is warning her that she has not studied for Friday's test.

rapid eye movement (REM) sleep—Also known as Stage 1 sleep, this is the time when a sleeper's eyes move beneath closed lids. Brainwave tracings confirm that the sleeper is dreaming at this time.

unconscious mind—The storehouse of feelings, thoughts, and memories that the mind keeps hidden. Dreams provide us with one of our few routes into the secret world of the unconscious.

on daily events, like walking to the store. Fears and worries take up more dreamtime than do happy feelings. If you remember a dream, it most likely occurred toward morning. That is when your dreams become more exciting. Best of all, dreams do not come to waste your time.

Beth Zimmerman's dream helped her resolve some bitter feelings. Several years after her father died, she dreamed about him. In the dream, her father turned his back on her. He seemed amused that she was trying to talk to him. At that point, Beth lost all control. The rage she had bottled up since his death poured out. Then she felt frozen with fear. What would he do or say? To her great relief, he looked at her and smiled. The smile warmed her heart and told her that he forgave her.

When she awoke, Beth thought about her dream. In life, she had not been able to tell her father how she felt. Now, thanks to the dream, she sensed that he truly had loved her. For the first time since his death, she felt at peace.[3]

Like Perry and Beth, your private "dream theater" is open. And the shows change nightly!

Dreaming Through History

Imagine a scene from the Stone Age. In the dark cave, Urgh sits up and rubs his eyes. He pokes his sleeping mate. "Oola, wake up," he orders. "I dreamed I was trampled by a woolly mammoth. What does it mean?"

No one knows what Oola told her mate, but we can be certain of two things. First, Urgh's sleep was filled with dreams. From lizards to lions, nearly all creatures dream.[1] Second, records show that humans have always wondered about their nightly "visions." Early peoples believed that the gods spoke to them in their dreams. Many went to tribal elders for help in decoding these messages. Other cultures studied dreams as a way of looking into the future. Will the harvest be fruitful? Should the tribe go to war? Tribal chiefs sometimes made life-and-death choices on the basis of a dream.

Even today, dreams play a central role in some cultures. The Senoi, who live in Malaysia, rely on dreams to shape their lives. A tribal leader called the Tohat ranks as the tribe's chief dream analyst. In the Senoi families, fathers serve as dream experts. Family members gather each morning to share the night's dreams.

A Senoi child told of a dream in which he fought with another boy. Today, his father said, you must give that boy a gift. This is one way the Senoi keep the peace. A girl told about her meeting with a dream lover. Next time, she was told, ask your lover for a poem or song. The song, she was told, will express the beauty of your love. Adult dreams often deal with larger problems. Thanks to one Tohat's dream, Senoi women gained equal rank with the men.[2]

The biblical story of Joseph is centered around a ruler's dreams. In ancient Egypt, the pharaoh relied on his wise men to interpret dreams. All was well until the wise men were stumped by two strange dreams. Troubled, the pharaoh called for Joseph, who was a skilled dream-worker. He told the Israelite he had dreamed of seven lean cattle that ate seven plump ones. Then in a second dream, seven thin ears of corn devoured seven fat ones.

According to the Bible, the pharaoh called on Joseph to interpret his troubling dreams. In this thirteenth-century illustration, Joseph (right, kneeling) speaks to the pharaoh (left).

Joseph warned the pharaoh that God had sent him a sign. "The land will have seven good years," he said, "followed by seven years of famine. Select a strong leader," Joseph urged. "Give him the task of planning wisely for the bad years to come."

The pharaoh was a good judge of men. He picked Joseph to prepare his country for the coming famine. It was a wise decision, for the Bible tells us that the pharaoh's dream did come true.[3]

Warning dreams turn up all through history. Calpurnia, wife of the Roman ruler Julius Caesar, dreamed of Caesar's statue. In her dream, she saw the marble statue bleeding from numerous wounds. She begged Caesar to stay home, but he ignored her. Later that day, his foes stabbed him to death as he entered the Roman Senate.[4]

Dreams can provide insights, too. Back in the 1800s, inventor Elias Howe's dream helped him solve a tricky problem. The insight he gained from the dream led to the invention of the sewing machine.[5] In another dream, Julia Ward Howe awoke with the words of a poem clear in her mind. Civil War troops were soon singing her dream poem as they marched to battle. Set to music, it became "The Battle Hymn of the Republic."[6]

In the 1800s, the chemist F. A. Kekulé was searching for the key to the structure of benzene. Then he had his famous "snake dream." He described the dream in these words: "Everything was moving in a snakelike and twisting manner. Suddenly one of the snakes got hold of its own tail and the whole structure was mockingly twisting in front of my eyes. As if struck by lightning, I awoke."

Julius Caesar is murdered in the Roman Senate by his enemies. Caesar's wife, Calpurnia, alarmed by a warning dream, had urged her husband not to go to the senate building that day.

Kekulé had spent years trying to solve the problem. Inspired by the "twisting snakes," he woke up knowing the answer. The benzene molecule, he realized, is shaped like a ring. Experts say that much of today's progress in organic chemistry began with Kekulé's dream.[7]

In 1964, an astromonkey named Bonny showed that animals dream, too. Bonny spent thirty days circling the earth in a satellite. All of her movements and reactions were taped. High above Chile, Bonny slipped into rapid eye movement (REM) sleep. The telltale brain waves told researchers that the astromonkey was dreaming.

Another study turned up REM sleep in myna birds, horses, gerbils, and raccoons. Dog owners say their pets howl and twitch in their sleep

The Sleepwalker

Outside, rain beat on the roof. A boy rose from his bed, eyes open and staring. Slowly, he walked through the house. He mumbled as he moved. Aroused by the noise, his parents watched him wander from room to room. Did they dare disturb him?

The boy opened the front door and slammed it behind him. Moments later his parents heard a loud knock. The boy was standing there, soaked to the skin—and wide awake. "How did I get here?" he asked. His dad told him that he had been sleepwalking. "I never sleepwalk," the boy said. With that, he changed his pajamas and went back to bed.

Scientists explain that the mind turns off the large muscles during dream sleep. In deeper levels of sleep, the body can be more active. If some part of the mind puts the body into gear, the sleeper moves around or calls out. Asked what's wrong, sleepwalkers often respond with nonsense statements. A teenager may mumble, "The cat needs gas." Complex actions, such as reading, are beyond the sleepwalker. Memories of sleepwalking "trips" vanish by morning.

Most sleepwalking stops by the late teen years. Except for keeping the child safe, parents need not worry about sleepwalking. Studies show that only a deeply disturbed person would commit a crime while asleep.

Sleepwalkers are usually young people.

after a stressful day. Perhaps they are dreaming about a trip to the vet. If awakened during REM sleep, cats often jump to their feet, looking fearful. Computer studies suggest that they may have been chasing "dream" prey.[8]

Your brain is far more complex than the brain of any dog, cat, or monkey. Better yet, you can remember your dreams. Dream experts say those weird and wonderful nighttime dramas have much to tell you.

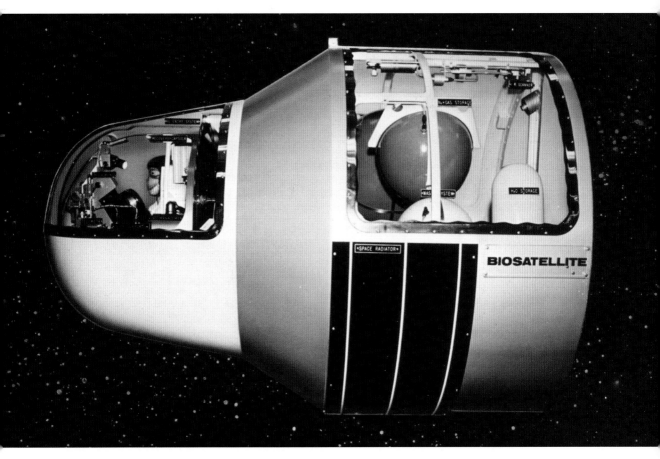

This is a model of a monkey strapped into the cabin of a satellite. While Bonny, one of the original astromonkeys, was orbiting Earth, researchers learned that animals dream, too.

Messages From Behind Locked Doors

Imagine a large iceberg floating in the Arctic Ocean. It looks so peaceful, sparkling in the sunshine. If you were a ship's captain, you would keep your distance. You would know that most of its huge bulk hides beneath the surface.

Your mind is like that iceberg. The "above-water" part (you're using it right now) is called the conscious mind. It controls all of your waking thoughts. Thinking about icebergs, for instance, is a task for the conscious mind. Like the iceberg, your mind also conceals a large submerged mass. Scientists call it the unconscious mind. A group of Scouts who survived a long-ago bus crash prove the point. Today, the former Scouts say they have forgotten that dreadful day. But studies show that the memory lives on, locked away in their unconscious minds.[1]

During your waking hours, the doors to the unconscious stay closed. But you cannot stay awake all the time. Your body and mind need sleep. Go too long without sleep and you will start to feel depressed. Your reaction time will slow down, and you will nod off at odd moments.

Sleep allows your body to catch up on its chores. Cells are repaired, and waste products cleaned out. A newborn baby sleeps twenty-two hours a day. Adults cut that to seven or eight hours.

The mind stays very busy while you are sleeping. As you move through the four stages of sleep, it sorts and files the day's memories. Every ninety minutes or so, you drift into Stage 1 (REM) sleep. This is when your dreams take center stage. The mind reaches back into the

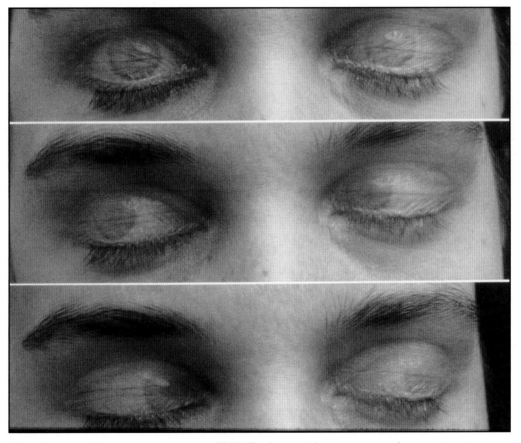

During rapid eye movement (REM) sleep, the eyes are in constant motion behind closed eyelids. People awakened during REM sleep often report that they were dreaming at the time.

unconscious to compose each night's dramas. Some dreams deal with current matters, such as school, family, and friends. Others relate to buried feelings. Toward morning, the dream periods increase in length.

Modern ideas about the meaning of dreams date back to Sigmund Freud. The Austrian neurologist first probed the unconscious in the late 1800s. In dreams, Freud said, the sleeper acts out deep-rooted needs and desires. He called this process "wish fulfillment." Strong wishes, he

Sigmund Freud believed that people act out their unconscious needs and desires in their dreams, a process known as "wish fulfillment."

added, can disrupt sleep. The mind conceals the real wish, therefore, as a dream symbol. You can see the process at work in twelve-year-old Tim's dream. Last night, Tim dreamed of driving a red sports car all over town. Is this a boy's wish to have his own car? Freud would dig deeper. Tim's dad, it turns out, keeps his son "grounded" much of the time. In the boy's dream, the sports car most likely stands for his wish to free himself from his parents' strict discipline.[2]

New theories soon followed. Carl Jung, Freud's great rival, said dreams can help us improve ourselves. He taught patients to search their dreams for clues about "lost" parts of themselves. Alfred Adler said that dreams can help us solve problems. In real life, you cannot try all the possible solutions. In dreams, you can test any idea, no matter how crazy.

Modern dream researchers build on the work that Freud began. Today, all across the United States, people talk of doing "dreamwork." Once they have captured a dream, they can study it for useful insights into their lives. Some meet with private counselors. Others join groups that share the task of decoding each member's dreams. One technique is to turn the dream into a drawing. A second is to keep a dream diary, either in a notebook or on a recorder.

Dreamworkers sometimes feel the urge to shout, "Aha!" That is the magic moment when the meaning of a dream becomes clear. The moment can come quickly, or it can take months of work. Carol Warner turned to dreams at a low point in her life. Each day for over a year, she studied her dream diary. Slowly, she began to see what she had to do.

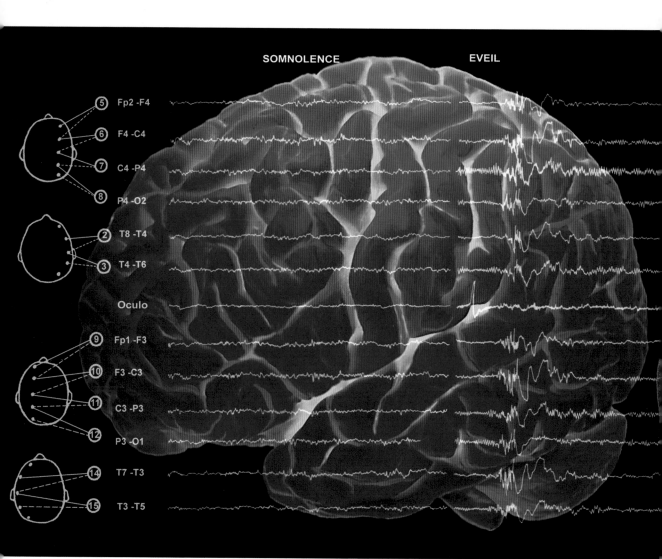

SOMNOLENCE   EVEIL

⑤ Fp2 -F4
⑥ F4 -C4
⑦ C4 -P4
⑧ P4 -O2
② T8 -T4
③ T4 -T6
Oculo
⑨ Fp1 -F3
⑩ F3 -C3
⑪ C3 -P3
⑫ P3 -O1
⑭ T7 -T3
⑮ T3 -T5

This chart shows the electrical activity that takes place in a person's brain during the inactive phase of sleep (left) and the beginning of the active phase of awakening (right). While sleeping, the brain is more active during its REM cycles.

Has Someone Been Stealing Your Dreams?

Okay, you say, so I dream every night. If that's true, why is it so hard to remember my dreams?

You are partly to blame. Once you wake up, dreams fade quickly. Thoughts of the day ahead drive them away. Catching those fast-fading dreams is like catching a butterfly. Quick movements and loud noises frighten the prey. You need to equip yourself with quiet, patience, and a notepad or recorder.

In the Western world, we often throw out our dreams like so much trash. Dream expert Ann Faraday puts much of the blame on our way of life. She says that most people treat dreams as frills. Parents, she adds, worry if their children neglect their schoolwork. They seldom scold Dick and Jane for skipping their dreamwork.

Faraday reminds us that many past cultures held dreams in high regard. There was a reason. From tiny fragment to scary nightmare, each dream has something to teach us. Unlock the dream gates, Faraday counsels. Once you do, you will never again be tempted to let your dreams slip away.[3]

The dreamcatcher (right), which originally came from the Ojibwa (Chippewa) Nation, is hung above the bed to protect a sleeping child from nightmares. The Ojibwa believe that a dreamcatcher can influence a person's dreams.

Over the next few weeks, she earned a promotion at work and split up with a boyfriend. For the first time in many months, she felt good about her life.[4]

Dreamwork can solve small problems, too. Jack Maguire was very nervous about visiting his stepsister. To gain insight into his feelings, he tried to interpret his dreams. Before he fell asleep, he stated the problem over and over. The technique worked. That night, he dreamed he gave his stepsister a flower. When he awoke, he knew that the flower was "a perfect gesture." Feeling relaxed at last, he carried a flower with him when he left for the airport.[5]

Ann Faraday, a leader in the field of dream analysis, preaches "dream power." Your dreams, she says, give you the power to take control of your life. If that sounds easy, think again. Most dreams resist analysis. Other people can offer advice, but only the dreamer can say, "Aha!" The unconscious does not give up its secrets without a struggle.

Dreams and the Psychic World

Can dreams foretell the future? Can you view distant events while you sleep? A.W. is convinced that her dreams unchained her own psychic powers. Her first taste of the power came when she was eight years old.

As a child, A.W. floundered while learning long division. Teachers and friends tried to help, but she could not master the skill. Then a dream came to her rescue. In the dream, the teacher called her to the chalkboard to work three long division problems. To her delight, A.W. solved the problems easily.

In school the next day, just as the dream predicted, A.W.'s teacher called on her. This time, the girl felt confident. She marched to the board, picked up the chalk, and worked the problems. In later years, she told friends that her "math dream" was the first of her psychic encounters.[1]

If A.W. is correct, dreams can touch upon the psychic world. Telepaths, for instance, claim they can send and receive messages without using any of the normal senses. In telepathic dreams, the dreamers believe they have received messages from someone else. Some of these dreams seem to zero in on real events. Others use symbols to disguise bad news.

A California grandmother awoke from a vivid dream. In the dream, she had seen her infant grandson tangled in a mound of blankets. Deeply disturbed, the woman quickly dialed her daughter's number. Her son-in-law answered. "Go to the baby at once," the woman said through her tears. "He's smothering."

"Not now, but he was," the surprised son-in-law replied. "Luckily, we were awake. We heard him thrashing around just in time."[2]

In a symbolic dream, the message comes through in a visual code. A San Francisco woman recalls a dream of this type. During World War II, her son Bill was sent to the South Pacific. In the dream, he walked in and held out his navy uniform. It was soaking wet. Bill looked distressed. "Isn't this terrible!" he said. Then he put his arms around her and sobbed.

A few days later, a navy chaplain arrived with terrible news. The woman's son and 250 shipmates had drowned when their ship went down. She checked the date. Bill had died on Monday, the night she wrote down her dream.[3]

A third type of psychic dream appears to launch the dreamer on an out-of-body experience (OBE). OBE dreamers claim to leave their bodies behind as they travel through time and space. They say they can look down on the bodies they left behind. During the OBE, they claim to float through walls and fly high above the earth. The dreamers say they see other people but seldom make contact.

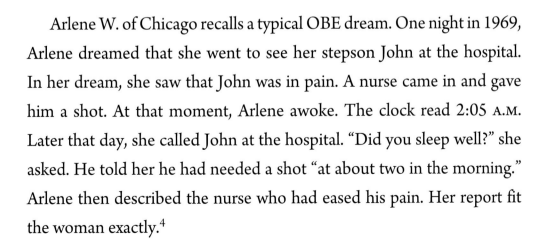

Sometimes dreams present their messages in the form of symbols. A San Francisco woman had a dream in which her son showed her his wet navy uniform and then fell crying into her arms. Later, the woman learned that her son had drowned the same night she had the dream.

Arlene W. of Chicago recalls a typical OBE dream. One night in 1969, Arlene dreamed that she went to see her stepson John at the hospital. In her dream, she saw that John was in pain. A nurse came in and gave him a shot. At that moment, Arlene awoke. The clock read 2:05 A.M. Later that day, she called John at the hospital. "Did you sleep well?" she asked. He told her he had needed a shot "at about two in the morning." Arlene then described the nurse who had eased his pain. Her report fit the woman exactly.[4]

Do psychic dreams really exist? Those who believe in them find all the proof they need in their own experiences. Science does not have that luxury. If psychic dreams are real, they must be tested under controlled conditions.

One research team uses *Ganzfeld* (German for "whole field") setups to lull the mind into a dreamlike trance. This allows for controlled testing of psychic powers. A team member first prepares thirty-six sealed envelopes. Each contains four pictures. The test begins as Anne leans back in a soft, comfy chair. With her eyes covered, she can see only a dim reddish light. Headphones pipe in the sound of gently breaking waves. A soothing voice helps her relax. Soon, her brain waves show that she has drifted into the desired dreamlike state. The voice tells her to focus on the thoughts that flit through her mind. The voice fades and the soft hiss of "white sound" fills her ears.

Half an hour later, Anne awakes and gives her report. "There was a road . . . a hard-packed pebble road," she says. "There was a fleeting image of being inside a car. . . . I had the feeling of driving out in the country, wide open areas, countryside landscapes."

The researcher opens one of the sealed envelopes. Anne does not know which picture has been picked as the "target." She flips past a Chinese painting, a still life, and a snow scene. The fourth shows a pickup truck cruising down a country road. "That's it," Anne says. "That's what I've been seeing."

Dream Skeptics at Work

In the 1960s, a sliding hillside of coal wastes buried a village school in Aberfan, Wales. Later, a number of people told of dreams that seemed to predict the disaster. At first glance, the stories appeared to show that precognitive dreams do exist. However, further study showed that the reports proved nothing. All of the reports came in after the event, not before.

A London newspaper saw a chance to run a test. It asked people to send in their precognitive dreams as soon as they had them. The paper received thousands of dreams during its fifteen-year test. A handful scored hits against real events. Experts were not impressed. The number of hits could be easily explained by the laws of chance.[5]

In 1965, a doctor dreamed of a long-lost friend. Moments later, the phone rang. It was his friend, calling from Hawaii. Surely, this was a psychic dream!

The doctor had second thoughts. Could the dream and the call be explained by coincidence? He worked out a formula based on three totals: friends, dreams, and phone calls received. The results showed that it was highly unlikely that his phone call happened by chance. His study also showed that it could happen to thousands of people every night.

Precognitive dreams, he judged, are like winning the lottery. Out of millions of players, someone is bound to win. It may feel like a psychic event but it's not.[6]

A woman relaxes in the glowing isolation of a Ganzfeld setup as researchers test her psychic powers.

The researcher smiles. Anne, from the depths of her dreamlike state, has scored a direct hit![7]

Despite Anne's success, the exact nature of ESP dreams remains in doubt. As with all ESP testing, skeptics often find fault with dream studies. For each "hit," there are an equal or greater number of "misses." Researchers cannot always repeat each other's results. However, like explorers mapping a strange land, ESP researchers move forward step by slow step.

CHAPTER FIVE

Making Sense of Your Dreams

You fall asleep as the clock strikes ten. Ninety minutes later, brain cells at the base of your skull begin to fire. Their impulses trigger a flood of memories. Now the mind can take over, weaving memories into a minifilm. Sometimes the script deals with events from the day just past. Often the images relate to deeper, more troubling feelings. Your private dream theater is open for a night's screenings.

When you awake in the morning, you remember one of your dreams. Should you write it down? Try to catch it before it fades, say the dream experts. Your dream scripts contain data drawn from the unconscious. Knowing those buried truths may help you solve problems, cope with feelings, and make choices.

Catching a dream is only the first step. The biggest step is trying to make sense of it. Some dreams, it turns out, mean what they say. Ruth R., who knows her brakes are bad, dreams of crashing her car. The manifest content of her dream is clear. Fix those brakes, Ruth, or you will have

Is Ruth's dream about a car accident telling her to fix her car's brakes, or is it a symbol that something else in her life is headed for a crash?

an accident. But what if Ruth's brakes are in fine repair? Then she must look at the dream's latent content—its symbolic meaning. Perhaps a new mall has been stealing customers from Ruth's flower shop. The dream may be warning that her business is heading for a crash.[1]

Roy T.'s dream helps prove the value of dreamwork. In the dream, Roy played basketball like a pro. Every shot he took swished through the net. Then a referee began calling him for foul after foul. Roy felt boxed in, unable to play his game. At last, feeling more and more frustrated, he took a close look at the referee. It was his mom!

The dream haunted Roy the next day. The manifest content did not help much. He seldom played basketball, and his mom was not a referee. But then the "Aha!" thought struck him. Roy had planned to go backpacking with a friend that summer. His mom wanted him to stay home to work with her. The dream, he realized, meant that she was "blowing the whistle" on his plans. Armed with that insight, Roy made a deal with his mom. He worked with her for a month—and then left for his trip.[2]

Roy had a dream about playing basketball. The referee in the dream was his mom. Roy had to look deep into the latent content of the dream before he could discover its symbolic meaning.

Warning Dreams: Ignore Them at Your Peril

When bad habits or poor choices threaten us, the mind may create a warning dream. Dream experts tell us it pays to stop for these flashing red lights.

Sleep researcher William Dement had a warning dream one night. In the dream, he saw a shadow on an X-ray of his lung. He knew it meant that he had cancer. A further check showed that the cancer was spreading. Remorse swept over him. He knew the cause of his coming death. Cigarettes! He should have quit smoking long ago. Dement awoke relieved to be alive. Acting on the warning, he quickly kicked his smoking habit.[3]

By ignoring her warning dream, June L. caused her son much pain. In her dream, two-year-old Dick was crying that his hip hurt. To her horror, she saw blood pouring down his leg. The dream troubled her, but her son seemed healthy at the time. It was a few months later that he began to drag his foot. A doctor found that the boy was bleeding internally at the hip. The cause was traced to a lack of vitamin C. Vitamin pills solved the problem, but not before Dick had suffered weeks of pain.[4]

Some dreamworkers use a process called lucid dreaming. Because they know they are dreaming during a lucid dream, they can take control of the action. The lucid dreamer says, "There is no way this nightmare can hurt me. It's only a dream. Let's see what happens if I face it." Perhaps the dream is one that recurs night after night. In that case, the dreamer can step in and add a happy ending.

Nancy used this method to cope with a recurring dream. In real life, she had been fighting with her mother. In her dreams, she and her son were attacked by a sharp-toothed digging machine. The night came, at last, when midway through the dream Nancy realized that she was dreaming. That gave her a chance to rewrite the script. Still in the dream, she turned to her son. The digger is a dream thing, she told him. It cannot hurt us. With that, the digger vanished. Nancy later dreamed that she was flying free, hand-in-hand with her son.

During a lucid dream, the dreamer takes control of the action. Nancy took charge of her dream, telling her son that the digging machine that was chasing them could not hurt them. At the end of her dream, Nancy and her son were flying happily hand-in-hand.

Dream Symbols

Drowning dreams are often symbols of depression or of something weighing you down.

Dreaming about money? It might be a signal to buy that new racing bike or gaming system.

A public nudity dream might mean you're worried about an upcoming challenge, such as an important math test.

Running scared in a dream? Try to focus on who (or what) might be chasing you.

A falling dream can be a warning—maybe your grades are "falling."

A flying dream may suggest that you've overcome a major challenge.

Nancy felt a sense of peace when she awoke. She now knew that the digger stood for her meddling mother. The insight took away her mother's power to hurt her.[5]

Some dream symbols are easy to decode. Have you ever had a falling dream? If so, it may mean that something in your life is "falling." It could be your grades, or a fall from favor with mom and dad. Once you know the cause, you can work to fix the problem. Flying dreams require that you look at the "feeling tone" of the dream. Did you feel carefree and happy? If so, perhaps you were "flying high" on the wings of a major success. Is something trying to drag you down during your flying dream? Look for a problem you have not been able to "rise above."

Another common dream finds you standing naked in a crowd. This is not a warning that you might do a strip-tease in public. It most likely stands for the worry you feel about a coming event. The solution? Be doubly prepared for the big game or the new school. Exam dreams can carry a similar message. First, you arrive late. Then you find you cannot answer any of the questions. For a student, the message is clear: Study harder for that big test. Adults have exam dreams, too. Their dreams often relate to the "tests" they face at work and at home.

Have you ever dreamed of finding a pile of money? Think of a money dream as a green light to move ahead with your plans. Or, if you have been feeling depressed, the dream may be sending a second message. It could be saying, "Cheer up! You are a good person!"

A Dreamcatching Expedition

Have you heard the old recipe for tiger stew? First, the wise hunter says, you must catch a tiger. That process applies to dreams, too. Do you want to analyze your dreams? First, you must catch them.

Dreamcatching is much safer than catching tigers. Here are the basic rules:

Rule 1. Keep a pen and paper, laptop, or some kind of recording device next to your bed. You must capture the dream before it fades.

Rule 2. Repeat over and over as you fall asleep, "Tonight, I will remember at least one dream."

Rule 3. Set an alarm clock to go off about four hours after you fall asleep. The goal is to wake up during or just after a REM cycle. If the first try does not work, reset the alarm for two hours later.

Rule 4. When the alarm goes off, sit up slowly. Turn on a dim light. If you have trapped a dream, write it down in as much detail as you can. Go through the process again when you wake up in the morning.

Want to catch your dreams? Keep a notebook and pen next to your bed and set your alarm to go off after a REM cycle would be ending.

Rule 5. Begin work on your dream analysis before you go to eat breakfast. Even if you do not finish, it is helpful to make a start while the dream is still fresh.[1]

Carla's sleep had been troubled for a week. That nightmare is trying to tell me something, she told herself. After two false starts, she caught the disturbing dream. The clock clicked over to 5:51 A.M. as she wrote down the details:

> I was in an orchard on a gray, cold day. I could see rows and rows of bare trees. Maybe there were elves sitting in the branches, but I could not be sure. The ground was slick, frozen hard. I felt

myself shiver. I looked down and saw that I was dressed in my pajamas. I felt myself blush. What if my friends saw me? Then I heard a loud droning noise. Moving toward me between the rows of trees was a giant snowman. Light flashed from its blue marble eyes. The droning noise seemed to be all around me. As I turned and ran, I could hear high-pitched voices laughing at me. At the end of the row, the trees held out their branches. The tangled branches blocked my flight. I screamed as the snowman came closer and closer. That was when I woke.

Carla worked on the dream that same morning. Clearly, she thought, this will be a tough one. She could see that the dream did not have much manifest content. At that point, she turned to a five-step process designed to help dreamcatchers analyze their dreams. After a few minutes of careful thought, she began to write.

Step 1: Recall recent events, which might be related to dream content. "The weather has been warm, not cold and wintry. School has been a drag, my history class most of all. I spent last weekend working in my uncle's orchard. Oh yes, I saw a Frosty the Snowman cartoon on TV last week. But Frosty is a friendly little guy, isn't he?"

Step 2: Discuss the "feeling tone" of the dream. "At first, I felt icy cold. I was embarrassed because I was dressed in pajamas. When the scary snowman chased me, I was frightened. Worst of all was the sound of the laughter. There I was, running for my life, and someone or something (the elves?) were laughing!"

Step 3: Identify the people you met in the dream. "I was the only real person in my dream. As far as I know, I was just myself. As for the

After Carla caught her dream, she had to figure out why the snowman was chasing her. She used a five-step process to analyze the dream.

elves, I keep thinking I know them. Could they be my classmates? The snowman was just a symbol, I guess. I'll work on it later."

Step 4: What do the dream symbols suggest to you? "Well, here's what I think:

Rows of trees—Familiar, yet strange; possibly machine-made.

Frozen ground—Smooth, almost polished.

Elves in trees—Mean, hard, cruel.

Pajamas—Exposed, wrong, makes me blush.

Snowman—White, white, white! Inhuman, fearful.

Blue marble eyes—They stared right through me.

Being laughed at—It hurt! I felt like I didn't belong.

Droning noise—Like bees buzzing; boring, not scary."

Step 5: Pull the dream together.

> I keep thinking of my problems with history. Ms. Thorn calls on me, and I never know the answers. Sometimes the other kids laugh at me. . . . Aha! That's it! The rows of trees are rows of desks. The elves are my classmates, most of whom I don't know very well. It's warm in the classroom, but I often feel cold because I'm nervous. Being caught in pajamas means I feel exposed to ridicule. As for the blue-eyed snowman, make it a snowwoman! Ms. Thorn has white hair and wears glasses with blue frames. And when she talks to us, her voice drones on and on. She never seems to change pitch.
>
> Let me sum up what the dream seems to be telling me. It looks as though I'm paying a heavy price for not doing my history homework. Snowwoman Thorn will chase me until I catch up with my reading. I'll start on it tonight![2]

Your dreams may carry messages of equal value. Are you ready to listen? Begin by catching as many dreams as you can. Jot them down in a private dream diary. Date each one so you'll know how it relates to the others. Don't worry if they do not make sense at first. Dreams do not give up their secrets easily. But neither do they come to waste your time. Why not join the thousands who use dreamwork to enrich their lives?

Chapter Notes

Chapter 1. This Theater Is Open Every Night

1. Marion Steele and Ronald Armstrong, *"I Had the Craziest Dream Last Night"* (Chicago: Nelson-Hall, 1971), p. 127.

2. Carl R. Green and William R. Sanford, *Psychology: A Way to Grow* (New York: Amsco School Publications, 1983), p. 39.

3. Reported to authors by a former student as part of a class project. "Beth" is a pseudonym.

Chapter 2. Dreaming Through History

1. Lyall Watson, *Supernature: A Natural History of the Supernatural* (London: Coronet Books, 1973), pp. 235–236.

2. Sol Gordon, *Psychology for You* (New York: Oxford Book Co., 1974), pp. 168–169.

3. The Bible, Genesis 41 (AV).

4. Will Durant, *Caesar and Christ* (New York: Simon & Schuster, 1944), p. 197.

5. Gayle Delaney, *Living Your Dreams* (New York: Harper & Row, 1979), p. 141.

6. Deborah Clifford, *Mine Eyes Have Seen the Glory* (Boston: Little, Brown, 1978), pp. 144–145.

7. Marion Steele and Ronald Armstrong, *"I Had the Craziest Dream Last Night"* (Chicago: Nelson-Hall, 1971), pp. 9–14.

8. Christopher Evans, *Landscapes of the Night: How and Why We Dream*, edited and completed by Peter Evans (New York: Viking Press, 1983), pp. 208–211.

Chapter 3. Messages From Behind Locked Doors

1. Carl R. Green and William R. Sanford, *Psychology: A Way to Grow* (New York: Amsco School Publications, 1983), pp. 167–168.

2. Ibid., p. 41.

3. Ann Faraday, *The Dream Game* (New York: Harper & Row, 1974), pp. 33–37.

4. Anastasia Toufexis, "Heavy Traffic on the Royal Road," *Time*, October 12, 1987, p. 76.

5. Ibid.

Chapter 4. Dreams and the Psychic World

1. Hans Holzer, *The Psychic Side of Dreams* (Garden City, N.Y.: Doubleday, 1976), pp. 103–104.

2. Richard Broughton, *Parapsychology: The Controversial Science* (New York: Ballantine, 1991), pp. 11–12.

3. Ibid., pp. 13–14.

4. Holzer, pp. 118–119.

5. Editors of Time-Life Books, *Psychic Powers* (Alexandria, Va.: Time-Life Books, 1987), pp. 32–34.

6. Ann Faraday, *The Dream Game* (New York: Harper & Row, 1974), pp. 314–316.

7. Broughton, pp. 99–101.

Chapter 5. Making Sense of Your Dreams

1. Reported to authors by a former student as part of a class project. "Ruth" is a pseudonym.

2. Carl R. Green and William R. Sanford, *Psychology: A Way to Grow* (New York: Amsco School Publications, 1983), p. 41.

3. Christopher Evans, *Landscapes of the Night: How and Why We Dream*, edited and completed by Peter Evans (New York: Viking Press, 1983), p. 233.

4. Hans Holzer, *The Psychic Side of Dreams* (Garden City, N.Y.: Doubleday, 1976), p. 91.

5. Ann Faraday, *The Dream Game* (New York: Harper & Row, 1974), p. 222.

Chapter 6. A Dreamcatching Expedition

1. Based on Ann Faraday's nine-step method as described in Carl R. Green and William R. Sanford, *Psychology: A Way to Grow* (New York: Amsco School Publications, 1983), p. 43.

2. Reported to authors by a former student as part of a class project. "Carla" is a pseudonym.

Glossary

conscious mind—The part of the mind that carries on a person's waking thought processes.

dream analysis—The process of trying to make sense of one's dreams.

dream symbols—Dream images that tend to hide their true meanings.

dreamwork—Catching and analyzing dreams.

extrasensory perception (ESP)—The ability to send or receive messages without using the normal senses.

Ganzfeld setup—An experimental technique that cuts subjects off from all sensory input so as to induce a relaxed, dreamlike state.

latent content—The hidden meaning of dreams, often concealed by dream symbols.

lucid dreaming—A technique in which subjects who are aware they are dreaming take control of their dreams. In lucid dreaming, dreamers write their own endings to dream scripts.

manifest content—Dream messages that can be taken at face value.

out-of-body experience (OBE)—A dream in which someone seems to leave his or her sleeping body behind while traveling to other places.

precognitive dream—A dream that seems to predict a future event.

rapid eye movement sleep (REM)—Also known as Stage 1 sleep, the stage of sleep during which dreams take place. During REM sleep, the sleeper's eyes move as if following the action of the dream.

sleepwalk—To perform simple actions such as walking while still asleep.

telepathic dream—A dream in which the sleeper seems to receive (or send) a message from (or to) another person.

unconscious mind—The storehouse of feelings, thoughts, and memories that the mind keeps hidden. Dreams provide one of the few routes into the unconscious.

warning dream—A dream that alerts the sleeper to danger.

white sound—Unvarying electronic "noise" that researchers use to screen subjects from distracting outside noises.

Further Reading

Books

Brynie, Faith Hickman. *101 Questions About Sleep and Dreams That Kept You Awake Nights—Until Now*. Minneapolis, Minn.: Twenty-First Century Books, 2006.

McCormick, Lisa Wade. *Psychic Powers*. Mankato, Minn.: Capstone Press, 2010.

Parks, Peggy J. *ESP*. San Diego, Calif.: ReferencePoint Press, 2008.

Rosen, Marvin. *Sleep and Dreaming*. Philadelphia: Chelsea House Publishers, 2006.

Scott, Elaine. *All About Sleep From A to ZZZZ*. New York: Viking, 2008.

Internet Addresses

Discovery Health: "How Dreams Work"
   <http://health.howstuffworks.com/mental-health/sleep/dreams/dream.htm>

Neuroscience for Kids—Sleep: What Is Sleep . . . and Why Do We Do It?
   <http://faculty.washington.edu/chudler/sleep.html>

Sleep for Kids—Teaching Kids the Importance of Sleep: Dreams
   <http://www.sleepforkids.org/html/dreams.html>

Index

A

Adler, Alfred, 21
animal dreams, 15–17

B

benzene, 14–15
Bonny, 15

C

Calpurnia, 14
conscious mind, 18
content types, 10
cultural roles of dreams, 12–14, 23

D

decoding dream messages, 12–14, 18–24, 31–38
definitions, 10
Dement, William, 34
dream analysis, 10, 28, 40
dreamcatchers, 23, 41
dream diaries, 21–24, 43
dreaming in color, 9
dream researchers, 9–11, 21
dreams generally, 7–11
dream symbols, 10, 21, 26, 32, 36–38, 42
dreamwork, 21–24, 39–43

F

Faraday, Ann, 23, 24
Freud, Sigmund, 20–21

G

Ganzfeld testing, 28–30

H

history of dreaming, 12–17
Howe, Elias, 14
Howe, Julia Ward, 14

I

insights from dreams, 14–15

J

Joseph, Egyptian pharoah, 13–14
Julius Caesar, 14
Jung, Carl, 21

K

Kekulé, F. A., 14–15

L

latent content, 10, 32
lucid dreaming, 34–38

M

manifest content, 10, 31–33, 41

O

out-of-body experiences, 26–27

P

precognitive dreams, 29

R

rapid eye movement (REM) sleep, 10, 15–17, 19–20, 39
remembering dreams, 23

S

Senoi, 12–13
sleep deprivation effects, 18–19
sleepwalking, 16
symbolic dreams, 13–14, 26

T

telepathic dreams, 25–26
"The Battle Hymn of the Republic," 14
theories of dreaming, 20–22

U

unconscious mind, 10, 18

W

warning dreams, 14, 32, 34, 38
wish fulfillment process, 20–21